THE PAST KEEPS CHANGING

BOOKS BY THE AUTHOR

POETRY
The Secrets of the Tribe

The Past Keeps Changing

TRANSLATION
A Dress of Fire: Poems by Dahlia Ravikovitch

Selected Poetry of Yehuda Amichai
(with Stephen Mitchell)

The Window: New and Selected Poems of Dahlia Ravikovitch
(with Ariel Bloch)

The Song of Songs
(with Ariel Bloch) (*forthcoming*)

CRITICISM
Spelling the Word: George Herbert and the Bible

For Raffaella
with warm wishes,

Chana Bloch
October 1995

THE PAST KEEPS CHANGING

CHANGING

poems by

CHANA BLOCH

The Sheep Meadow Press
Riverdale-on-Hudson, New York

All inquiries and permission requests should be addressed to: The Sheep Meadow Press, P. O. Box 1345, Riverdale-on-Hudson, New York 10471.

Distributed by Independent Literary Publisher's Association
P.O. Box 816
Oak Park, IL 60603

This book has been composed in Linotron Bembo

Typeset and printed by Princeton University Press on acid-free paper. It meets the guidelines for permanence and durability of the Committee on Production Guidelines for Book Longevity of the Council on Library Resources.

Library of Congress Cataloguing-in-Publication Data

Bloch, Chana, 1940-
   The past keeps changing : poems / by Chana Bloch.
      p.   cm.
   ISBN 1-878818-15-5 (acid-free) : $10.95
   I. Title.
PS3552.L548P3   1992
811'.54—dc20
                                                    92-9628
                                                       CIP

for my mother

CONTENTS

I

The Family   3
The Valley of the Dead   4
Primer   7
Talking Back   10
Thanksgiving   11
Thirteen   12
The Lesson   13
Chez Pierre, 1961   14
Goodbye   15
The Past We Keep   16
Our Lives from Above   17
Fingerprints   18
Duck/Rabbit   19
Listening   20
Deadwater   22
White Ink is for Memory   23
Noli Me Tangere   24
Exile   27

II

Crossing the Table   31
White Petticoats   32
Little Love Poem   33
Eating Babies   34
Real Life   37
Hunger   38
The Ghost Worm Monster   39
Night Shift   42
Inside   43
Firewood   44
The Stutter   45
Eclipse   48
Against Gravity   49

The Captive   52
Rising to Meet It   53
Changeling   54
Blue–Black   55
Wherever You Are   56
The Physics of Distance   57
Anniversary   58

III

Mama Pudding   61
Practicing   62
Learning Fire   63
Milkweed   64
At the Open Grave   65
Vision   66
In the Land of the Body   67
Alone on the Mountain   75
Deaths I Come Back To   76
Day–Blind   77

ACKNOWLEDGMENTS

I wish to thank the editors of the following publications, where these poems first appeared (some in earlier versions, or with different titles):

BRIDGES: *White Ink is for Memory*

FIELD: *Primer, Listening, Deadwater, Little Love Poem, Hunger, In the Land of the Body* (parts 2 and 6)

THE IOWA REVIEW: *Thirteen, Crossing the Table, Anniversary*

IRONWOOD: *The Valley of the Dead, The Stutter, Night Shift, At the Open Grave*

PLOUGHSHARES: *Alone on the Mountain, Deaths I Come Back To*

POETRY: *The Family, Chez Pierre, 1961, White Petticoats, The Ghost Worm Monster, Inside, The Captive, Against Gravity* (part 2), *Rising to Meet It, Blue-Black, Mama Pudding, In the Land of the Body* (parts 3, 5 and 8)

POETRY NORTHWEST: *In the Land of the Body* (parts 1, 4 and 7)

SOUTHERN POETRY REVIEW: *Learning Fire*

SOUTHERN REVIEW: *Milkweed*

The Lesson, Goodbye, Exile, Eating Babies, Firewood and *Vision* appeared in THE SECRETS OF THE TRIBE (The Sheep Meadow Press, 1981).

I am very grateful to the National Endowment for the Arts for a Fellowship in Poetry, and to the Djerassi Foundation, the Mac Dowell Colony and Yaddo, where some of these poems were written. Many dear friends have read the poems and offered valuable suggestions; I particularly want to thank Tess Gallagher, Shirley Kaufman and Stanley Moss, whose comments changed the shape of this book. My greatest debt is to Anita Barrows, who watched it evolving week by week and helped immensely with her clear-eyed responses.

I

This is from where
my strength comes, even when I miss my strength
even when it turns on me
like a violent master.

—*Adrienne Rich, "Sources"*

THE FAMILY

INSIDE the Russian woman there's
a carved doll,
red and yellow to match her,
with its own child inside.
The smallest, light as a saltshaker,
holds nothing
but a finger's breadth of emptiness.

Every morning we are lifted
out of each other,
arms stiff at our sides.
In the shock of daylight
we see our own
varnished faces everywhere.

At night we drop back
into each other's darkness.
A tight round sky
closes over us
like a candle snuffer.

We sleep
staring at the inside.

THE VALLEY OF THE DEAD

in memory of H.

1

NO ONE feeds the dead anymore.
No one leaves them juniper berries and melon seeds
in an alabaster bowl.
They have stopped hunting in the ochre marshes.

They used to live forever
on painted wheat.
The sky was flat; the sun skimmed across it
in a boat. At that latitude

there is no twilight. The gods
with their beaked hunger—
falcon, jackal, hawk—
wait, enormous, on the walls.

2

IN THE LONG leisure
of heaven

there is no friction, the hand
goes on waving the fan of ostrich feathers,

the ivory bird is called back
as witness

and the chairs with their stiff
clawed feet. Nothing

happens only once.
We perform the past over and over

until we get it right.

3

WHATEVER you gave me, I used it up right away
for breathing.
That's why nothing is left but amulets,
red paint flaking off the potsherds,
Isis holding out her naked breasts
in both hands—

your hands. Sun edges in
the broken shutter—
                              The rest
turned into body and bread.

The pain is historical, silted under
other sediments,
and it doesn't hurt.

Whatever you gave me, I made it serve,
I couldn't save it
for later. That's why only your handprints
are left, faintly visible,
pressed into the clay.

PRIMER

1

ON THE kitchen table, under
a dusting of flour, my mother's hands
pressed pastry into the fluted shell
with experienced thumbs.

Mustard-plaster, mercurochrome wand,
blue satin binding of the blanket
I stroked to sleep,
soft tar roof where the laundry
bellied and bleached,
sky veined with summer lightning:

If we were so happy,
why weren't we happy?

2

DREAMS sink a deep shaft down
to that first shoe,
bronzed, immortal.

We looked up at a sky of
monumental nostrils, grim tilted
backlit faces.

We learned to shape the letters,
l's and t's looped and tied, small i's
fastened by a dot.

When we stood up, our feet reached the ground.
We wiped the kisses from our cheeks with the back of our hands.

3

I THOUGHT I was a grasshopper
in the eyes of giants.
My father set his hand on the doorknob,
slowly, without looking at me;
my mother lifted her hand, the fingertips
Hot Coral.
I thought she was saying Come here.

That's why I kept calling them back: *Look,*
look who I've become!
But it was too late;
he had his jacket on, and she
was smiling at her mouth in the hall mirror.

Now I am huge. This is my
bunch of keys, my silence, my own
steep face. These
are my children, cutting on the dotted lines:
blunt scissors
and a terrible patience.

TALKING BACK

for my mother

YOU DON'T tell it right, either. And you were
there with your clever fingers from
the beginning. When you printed
my mouth on your cheek, and crooned: *She's
kissing me.* When you made your voice small
as a sparrow's, and sang: *How I love*

my Mommy. O master
ventriloquist, yes.
Yes, it was good. Very good. It was horrid.

The deadbolt of evening.

But when I tell it, I always leave out
the soft-boiled egg you set
on the bedside table, the satin
talcum powder, the little fringed terry-cloth robe
after the bath.

Your rhinestone earrings, your hatpins, the red-knobbed
radio laughing
on Sunday afternoons as the sun
coasted down the sky—

Yes, mother, I saved them. I braided the good past
into the bad till it grew
long, lustrous, tough. And let it down
hand over hand through the dormer window,
slow, down the slippery wall.

THANKSGIVING

"GOLD CANDLESTICKS," Miss Bye explained.
"That's why the pilgrim fathers ran away to America!
That's why we're here."
We were painting the turkey wattles red. Our parents
would be proud.

But if there's a soul,
where is it? we asked each other, dipping
our brushes in the paint.

Rachel said, *Inside your head, in your brain,*
a kind of thin cloud.
Annie said, *In your heart. No one knows for sure.*
Or maybe it shifts around, I thought.
Like invisible blood.

We were building log cabins out of cardboard
with cellophane smoke curling up through the roof.
Last week we did the Indians:
succotash, rain-dance, tobacco,
plant-fish-in-the-ground-to-make-it-fertile.

Miss Bye said, "Wash out the brushes when you're done,
and be quick about it." An autumn gray
fogged the tall windows. The air was damp:
tempera paint and galoshes.

I loved the scars on my slanted desk, I was glad
for the inkwell. I could almost feel
the soul in my fingertips
shiver; no, under my tongue.

THIRTEEN

NOBODY KNOWS how serious it is
to have such small breasts.
No one knows what you pray for.

You're eating tomatoes, still warm
from the yard, the juice
running down your face.

How the ripe ones ooze
to your finger's push,
spill themselves

over your hands.
How the flat sun throbs
whenever you

watch it hard. You want
the sun with its green
afterprint, those

sticky salts
drying to a glaze,
you want to lie pressed to

a pounding heart.
Now stare back until it hurts.
You won't be first

to look away. The heat
reaches inside your shirt.
It sees everything.

THE LESSON

WHEN SHE played
those veins
glittered and jumped.

That's what I saw
from the piano bench
under the tasselled lamp—

and in the back room that scarecrow
her mother, dirty rouge
on the cheekbones, the hooded eyes
staring.

Each Tuesday I'd come back,
tugging at my music:
*Will I have veins like that
when I learn to play?*

The ugliness of the adult world,
how I craved it—
not knowing but wanting.

"What a man
does to a lady"—whatever I dreamed
that mystery would be like,

the brutal music
of a real life,

bent over kissing
hair, breastbone, thigh,

whatever could make her blood
stand up like that.

CHEZ PIERRE, 1961

THE SKIRT'S all wrong and the shoes
hurt: thin straps
and little pointed heels. Borrowed clothing.
She crosses her legs under the table. No.
Uncrosses them.

Heat rises heavy, a raincloud
gathering moisture.
His hand comes down over hers.
All those couples, look! their lives
are already a downpour.

She can't imagine me yet, though she's starting
that puzzled
tuck around the mouth, the one I'm
only now getting used to.
He draws little O's on her palm

with a dab of finger, laughing, taking
his time. I still
carry her with me, unfinished,
into the hazard
of other people's hands,

I live with her choices.
The waiter says, "Sweet?
or dry?" and wipes the dew from a bottle.
She's got to decide, *now!*
for my life to begin.

GOODBYE

THE REPAIR MAN in the doorway,
yellow hard-hat, scrub-jacket: *Goodbye.*
He slips back into his life with
a fence around it.
Draped windows. Not mine.

Lately I am so hard
people keep sliding off me.

This emptiness sharpens me.
Light prints itself on the plate of memory,
acid burned into metal.

It's thirty years since you and I invented
a ritual for leaving.
Back to back in the city street,
we walked five paces apart and were swallowed up
by our lives.

When they said, "If you eat this fruit
you will die,"
they didn't mean right away.

THE PAST WE KEEP

for Martin, after 30 years

I SAVED the tree where we hung our clothes
and the rasp of little twigs under us.
You kept the ferry ride, wild with salt.
Blue-green days
we planted once, like flags.

The island grows larger and larger as it swerves,
all stinging spray, away from us.

I want to put out a hand to touch
that knobby bone in your chest
the way I used to—

We're in your house, a laundry basket
between us
to keep us chaste.
I'm folding my sons' T-shirts into careful squares.

Why didn't we? you ask, and we're
inside the brilliant heat again,
almost, as if it were still gathering
moment by moment, as if the blues and greens
were still lifting, plunging
in an unpredictable wind.

Your daughter walks into the room,
blond, holding her guitar.
Again I discover
she doesn't look like me.

OUR LIVES FROM ABOVE
for Rachel

THESE OCHRES and golds, strung out to dry
in a strong sun,
were once, when we loved the same man,
our lives. He was a different place
for each of us: shoulder of road,
flank of mountain.

What we live from moment to moment
encloses us: the phone booth
at the corner drugstore, airtight and severe
as a Shaker cupboard,
the sticky grip of the receiver, the pile of dimes.
Where was he, that night?
I couldn't find my way to the next sorrow.

Now it's the two of us
idling over the countryside, just high enough
to see pattern and color.
Everything looks ordained
at this altitude, proportioned, as if we did only
what we had to do,
like roads that follow the curve of a riverbed.

"If he loves you"—spiky words, ink
on onionskin. How I hated
that letter! And he, twisting your ring
from his finger, giving it to me.

The sun has scrubbed the hills
to a soft worn suede.
One by one, we find the letter, still
folded, the wishbone,
the narrow ring,
and give them back to each other.

FINGERPRINTS

CYPRESS TREES on Colusa
where I stop on a hot day and smell
Jerusalem. Cobbles. Green dust.

Not what he told me but his crooked tooth.
Not that gaunt winter but the back
of his neck
and his wrinkled sheets.
Whiskey and toothpaste. He left
clues all over me.

I take my books from the liquor cartons
and run a rag down the bindings, the
speckled bellies. An intimate gesture.
I've carried them back and forth across the Atlantic
and never opened them.

Late afternoon is a cone of dust-motes.
I'm falling asleep
from the footsoles up. Cold pinpricks, a swarm
of small deaths. When the sun goes down
I'm breathing the dust of myself.

Everything happens only once but
I go on asking, and asking is
the quickest way back.

DUCK/RABBIT

*We remember the rabbit when we see
the duck, but we cannot experience
both at the same time.*
— *E.H. Gombrich,* Art and Illusion

WHAT *do you remember?* When I looked at
his streaky glasses, I wanted
to leave him. *And before that?* He stole those
cherries for me at midnight. We were walking
in the rain and I loved him.
And before that? I saw him coming
toward me that time at the picnic,
edgy, foreign.

But you loved him? He sat in his room with
the shades drawn, brooding. *But you
loved him?* He gave me
a photo of himself at sixteen, diving
from the pier. It was summer. His arms
outstretched. *And before that?*
His mother was combing his soft curls
with her fingers and crying. Crying.

Is that what he said? He put on the straw hat
and raced me to the barn. *What did he
tell you?* Here's the dried rose, brown
as tobacco. Here's the letter that I tore
and pasted. The book of blank pages
with the velvet cover. *But do you still*

love him? When I rub the nap
backwards, the colors lift,
bristle. *What do you mean?*
Sometimes, when I'm all alone,
I find myself stroking it.

19

LISTENING

IT'S YOUR dream, not mine. That's why
we're all in one place:
you, me, your dead wife,
your mistress, your girlfriend, everyone's
puzzled children.

We climb on the carousel without speaking.
Then Lenore is there, with a suitcase.
So she's back, after all.
The horses are chipped, forelegs tensed
for distance,
stiff tails lifted in an imagined wind.

The children wave, sticky-fingered, in case
anyone is looking. If they could speak
they'd say: *Choose.*
The horses obey the law of the circle.

This is your dream. You wrote it. That's why
the women lean forward in their stirrups as if
to kiss each other, and the children
close their eyes. They're so young,
aren't they? Your voice
pauses over this, choosing

where to slow down. It is, after all,
your dream. Pretty soon
your wooden horse will grow warm,
whinny, throw back its head, leap out

into the green. Why are you
telling me this, suddenly happy,
tapping the spoon against the spongy
palm of your hand? Why
am I leaning forward, listening,
like one of them?

DEADWATER

WHAT STIRS it up from the muck again,
forty years' worth,
just when I was able to see
enlarged in water
the tangled stems at the bottom?

My mother sits in the rowboat, head down,
hands closed around nothing.
"You never loved me," she starts, and
looks up suddenly.
Or did I say it?

I work the boat up and down
the scummy lake, skirting the lily pads:
flat green waxy hearts
on their long strings.

Reach down with a forked stick, one touch
and the ghost
swirls and rises, a cloud of silt endlessly
raining itself out. Look

how it settles down, pretends
to be solid.

WHITE INK IS FOR MEMORY

in memory of Ida Bloch
(b. 1903, Heidelberg—d. 1981, Haifa)

YOUR MOTHER found her bosom too large
in the photograph.
She looked at it, frowning. One hand
tugged at the front of her dress.

Strangers live in the house where she was born.
She saved this album for you:
the Rathaus from her window,
a field and a family
she put away like embroidered linens.
Everyone on the back porch is pressed flat
between these pages.

She alone escaped to remember
her grandfather at the pianola like a stuffed
Paderewski, the high C of windowglass
shattering, the prize canary
huddled in its cage.

Even loss grows supple from this far away,
a round we all sing with its aching
diminished sevenths.

Those leathery aunts, sleeked
by the airbrush that softens
whatever it touches.
Hatbrim, whisker and dewlap, they sit
at the wicker table,
Berta, Sophie, Tante Johanna.

NOLI ME TANGERE

1

THE MAN at the corner looks like my
dead father. That tightness
around the eyes. He steps off the curb and
I almost stop him
—a stranger, waiting to cross a street
in his own life.

I make him speak
without his knowing it.

2

AND YOU: what I take is not
what you give me, either.
I stall at the window, drawing
a face in steam. *Why did you tell me?*
Don't go. You, quick on the thread of
wherever you're going. Silent,
you close your eyes

the way my father used to. God
of the supper table, hoarding
his words. And I, at the iron
edge of my chair. Any child knows
how to make a feast
of crumbs and silence.

3

THE PAST we started hasn't
finished with us. It chooses a body,
a bait, a jacket
wet in the rain. O my tower
of newspaper, pillar of
smoke—
How the light flashed
from his rimless glasses! I am still trying
to make him look up.

EXILE

WHAT HAPPENED to the ten lost tribes
is no great mystery:
they found work, married, grew smaller,
started to look like the natives
in a landscape nobody chose.
Soon you couldn't have picked them out of a crowd.

And if they'd stayed where they were,
what happiness
would they have endured?
We can't believe in it.

The face of the cities scares us,
day and night empty us, suddenly
we are no longer
God's chosen.

    We salvage
a pewter dish cross-hatched as a bubba's face,
a bent spoon. But the sober

dance of the mouth and the eyes before
we knew we were smiling, a language
stripped and intimate—

For a while we camp out under the strange trees,
complaining, planning a return.
But we have taken out papers and will become citizens.

II

We are the instruments of a hard love.
—*Yehuda Amichai, "Instead of Words"*

CROSSING THE TABLE

THAT OLYMPIC couple on ice
with their satin swoopings.
No, it's not ease I'm after.

I hate table talk *Pass the
salt, tomorrow rain.* Goodbye
tired bodies trading clichés.

I want the language of lovers before
they touch out loud,
when their eyes telegraph
verbs only, because
each word costs.

The way they startle and
contract: have they given away
too much too soon?

Across the table
you're a foreign city
where the natives always talk fast.

A whole swarming life to tell, no time to
tease the words out, crazy
to connect, we
strain like children breaking

into speech.
                        You look up: I
step out in frantic English
into the traffic.

WHITE PETTICOATS

for Ariel

IF THE EGG had one spot of blood on it
the rabbis said, Throw it away!
As if they could legislate
perfection.
Dress the bride in white
petticoats! Let there be

no stain
on your ceremony! As if
we could keep our lives
from spilling
onto our new clothes. That night
we came home

strangers, too tired
for words,
fog in the high trees
and a trunk full of shiny boxes
we didn't unwrap.
There's a bravery

in being naked.
We left our clothes
on the doorknob, the floor, the bed,
and a live moon opened its arms
around the dark.

LITTLE LOVE POEM

RAIN FRECKLES the path.

In the meadow, raw
upturned earth.
Zebra-legged birches riding
into the wind.

Tiny explosions of happiness:
tight-fisted lilacs
bursting
their purple pods.

EATING BABIES

1

FAT
is the soul of this flesh.
Eat with your hands, slow, you will understand
breasts, why everyone
adores them—Rubens' great custard nudes—why
we can't help sleeping with
pillows.

The old woman in the park pointed,
Is it yours?
Her gold eye-teeth gleamed.

I bend down, taste the fluted
nipples, the elbows, the pads
of the feet. Nibble earlobes, dip
my tongue in the salt fold
of shoulder and throat.

Even now he is changing,
as if I were
licking him thin.

2

HE SQUEEZES his eyes tight
to hide
and blink! he's still here.
It's always a surprise.

Safety-fat,
angel-fat,

steal it in mouthfuls,
store it away
where you save

the face that you touched
for the last time
over and over,
your eyes closed

so it wouldn't go away.

3

WATCH HIM sleeping. Touch
the pulse where
the bones haven't locked
in his damp hair:
the navel of dreams.
His eyes open for a moment, underwater.

His arms drift in the dark
as your breath
washes over him.

Bite one cheek. Again.
It's your own
life you lean over, greedy,
going back for more.

REAL LIFE

AT MIDNIGHT, invisible, I give
and I take away, reaching
under my son's pillow.

He leaves a trail of teeth
and I follow it. When supper comes
I set the table, fat spoon

and knifeblade,
serve up a dish of steam
and tell him: Eat.

I am what I am,
he believes in me.
"But does she *really* come

in real life? Does she?"
He kicks the leg of the table
idly, writes

his name in spilt milk.
The new teeth are always sharp,
tipped with three points

that eating eats away.
He picks up the quarter, rubs it
between his fingers,

bites down hard.

HUNGER

WHAT GOES OUT into the world in boots
comes back
banging a spoon on the scarred table: *More.*

Day comes back dusk, was it
brightness you wanted?

You go out full. Night
brings you home again, dragging
a sack of emptiness.
And what did you ask for, woman?
Manna, six-pointed, glimmering
its little beads of honey?

This is the house that was carved for you
from a single beam of cedar.
The meal is set,
a wreath of steam on the white cloth.

You've had your seven wishes
and never been grateful.
When all this
vanishes

you'll be back
in that hovel by the sea,
sweeping the bare stones.

THE GHOST WORM MONSTER

1

THE CHILD is gathering sticks
and stones, hard pits of
words he can't
take into his mouth yet, zigzag
cracks in the sidewalk, blades of pointy
green pushing through.

Musk of his pillow, drift and sway
of the lazy dust motes.
Nobody's looking.

He's saving bits of me, too. Like string.

2

HURRYHURRY, *she said. But why*
were her eyes so

angry, why was her face
so mean. How could the light

fall from the ceiling and find
the broken saucer. Why did she yell

Enough. *Why did she*
run from the room, holding

a towel. Why does the water
swirl in the sink, faster,

faster. Where is it going, where

3

THE CHILD startles awake.
The ghost worm monster, he stammers,
sitting up. And won't
go back to sleep.

I run a hand down the sloping
shoulderblades, little wishbones
of balsa wood.
Did I come out of you? he says. That dream
came out of him.

The time he was lost, I kept
sending his name
to look for him. Day shut
on iron hinges;
the light drained out of it.

I want him buttoned around me
against the cold
                    the way he wants
to float inside me again,
swaddled in water.

NIGHT SHIFT

ALL NIGHT, in the cramp of sleep,
we grind the day-stone between our molars,

we spin
straw into flesh.

It is a form of penance. Locked
in our bodies,

our legs unstrung.
The bed is crowded: you

in your striped pajamas,
me, pillow feathers

with their memories of flight.
Your dreams and mine rise to the ceiling and

hang there, looking
down at us

till we beg: Come back, come back inside us,
it's almost morning.

INSIDE

IS IT BLUE
inside a bluebird? the child said.

Then he told me: A baby's head is all stuffed
with hair. It keeps growing out, frizzy,
till it gets used up. That's why
old men are bald.

FIREWOOD

WHEN YOU SAWED a branch from the pine tree
the white sky submerged us,
a clear fluid brisk as vinegar, and I kept
missing it, kept going out to look at
what I knew wasn't there.

Put it back! I begged, but the branch
was already a pile of logs, wrist-thin,
paler inside than our child's face.
One evening's wood.

The luxury of that low branch hanging down!
We had to duck every time to get past,
it choked out the sun,
nothing but pine needles grew under it.

In the fire I see our own faces
losing their shape.
There's no way to change
without touching
the space at the center of everything.

THE STUTTER

1

WE SPEAK too fast.
The child sits at our table, waiting
his turn. The clock
points a sharp finger. The daily
soup steams,

too hot to eat. Between
words the child thrashes *I-I-I*—
Our patience

takes a deep breath.

2

THAT HIGH VOICE—all clumsy fingers—
can't untie
the shoelace fast enough. The master of the house
is counting. The hurt
voice circles
over and over, blunt needle picking at an old
blocked groove.

3

YEARS AGO in a high chair
he drummed wet fists, his face
a knot: *Give me*
words. The fury
beat in his throat. Mother and father, we put
words in his mouth, we

speak harder, faster, we give him
a life to chew on.

ECLIPSE

THERE ARE two bodies floating above us:

They are one body,

yours dark, a silence

tails of flame lashing the emptiness,

growing in space,

emptiness opening its mouth wide

mine a ring of fire clenched around it.

to swallow the fire.

AGAINST GRAVITY

1

NOVEMBER. A forty-watt twilight.
You bring me the white of your face
like a letter with an old address,
so rubbed out I can't
decipher it.

I watch you stare up
at the naked prongs of the fig tree.

You're secreting a silence around you,
iridescent, slippery. I don't know
where the body stops and the outer
darkness begins.

Remember last spring? It was you
who showed me,
pointing up, laughing:
caterpillars held by invisible
threads in the branches,
doing their little dance against gravity.

2

I CARRIED the child for weeks without telling,
letting the secret
feed me. Only you and I knew
and we closed

around each other. I grew a path
we could take without needing
to speak. Light passed between us
at midnight, poured

from a cloudy source and kept
pouring.

3

IN THE HARD light, we study
each other's faces
like the deaf.

When we cut down the pine
we read its story
in the plain script of trees: drought years
and flood years. It's all clear

afterward. At the center the dead
heartwood with its
five cracked spokes. Then the pitted bark,
that keeps things out.

THE CAPTIVE

THE BODY carves itself
with its own hand,
leaves crude incisions
around the mouth, the eyes.

But the stone wants only
to lie down
in its plot of shadow. Wants
not to be touched.

RISING TO MEET IT

PAIN IS the salty element.

All that night I lay
tethered to my breathing. To the pain,
the fixed clock-stare of the walls,
the fingers
combing my tangled hair.
Ride out the waves, the doctor said.

The first time I touched a man,
what startled me more than the pleasure
was knowing what to do.
I turned to him with
a motion so firm it must have been
forming inside me
before I was born.

I was swimming upstream, the body
solid, bucking for breath, slippery,
wet. An ocean
rolled off my shoulders.

Tonight, strapped to the long night, I miss
the simple
pain of childbirth—
                            No, not the pain
but that rising to meet it like a body
reaching out in desire, buoyant, athletic,
sure of its power.

CHANGELING

THROUGH the half-open door I can hear it
in the other room, breathing.
Branches on glass, a cold blade
scraping my backbone.
It won't go away.

One eye like a knot of wood, staring,
one eye torn with rain.
I am yours, it says.
You will learn to live with me.

I beg the window: Be morning.
This is still my house.

It stirs, turns over, pulls at the dark.
It always wakes with a cry.
How eagerly its craving flares
at my footsteps.
I take it to my breast
and let it bite.

BLUE-BLACK

THAT ROAD leads only
to the bridge, to the
hiss and slap
of water, the muddy
suck of the bottom.
I know the way.

All winter
I pitched through night in a fury of falling,
falling,
wind in my teeth,
my body an old coat with stones
in its pockets.

I found my body on the bridge.
Fingers locked to the cold rail,
counting, as if
the blue-black
slippery ocean were a hope
to hang onto.

I knew that old coat,
the brown shag, the missing
buttons. I watched
my slow fingers
choosing. My knuckles.
My stubborn feet.

WHEREVER YOU ARE

NOW YOU'RE home again, shaving; you stand
at the open window, whistle
a little song to yourself;
walk across the room. I'm making you up

so real you bump into a chair
and stop, puzzled, rubbing
your knee. *Now you're at the lake, hurrying*
toward me. My hand
reaches through you,
dangles, silly. . . .

I let it sink. The water startles and
comes back different.

But where would we go then? I ask
the lake. Nothing here but old houses,
upside-down
like the roots of houses.
                                And that face
in the water: something keeps snagging
behind the eyes, a tangle
of algae stirring the surface, the nudge
and boil of
something borne away.

THE PHYSICS OF DISTANCE

MISSING YOU, I touch my face in the mirror.
It's formal, serious,
as in those old sepia photos before smiling
came into fashion.

Cool and slippery under the question mark
of my palm print, I live alone
in the shallow mirror, framed
in pale oak.

I've lost a dimension. Maybe distance
is a kind of innocence.

Who was I, before I knew you?
I used to save pain,
I used to think everything we said was indelible.

Where you are, it's still afternoon.
I put on the earrings you gave me,
the silver earrings,
and tilt my head in the mirror, a young girl's
invitation.

ANNIVERSARY

THE METAL GATE has a crow-cry, almost human.

You'll see, said the elders, speaking
in riddles.

Twenty years, in October.
I stroke the rise of your cheek like a talisman:
sun and wind scored in the dusty ground
of our faces.

              These planted
fenceposts, the scaling, the crude joins, the cankered
nails. The sawed-off rounds of the woodpile,
seasoned, waiting
to be used. The feathered seedpod
rolling over and over across the road on its white floss.

Your hand on my shoulder, like a question—

Rosin of sunlight slides up and down
a string of spiderweb,
bowing a high note. The eye
can hear it.

III

I wish I understood the beauty
in leaves falling. To whom
are we beautiful
as we go?

—*David Ignatow, "Three in Transition"*

MAMA PUDDING

YOU HAVE SEVEN gray hairs, says my son, my
firstborn,
and lifts me off the floor.
Pokes an accusing thumb into
Mama Pudding,
fixes a beam of truth and refuses
to gentle it.

At his age, I'd scour
my elbows with half a lemon
to make them white as a lady's.

My mother sagged in her casing.
Her dress was too bright, her eyelids
gleamed like fish-scales.
I tried on her crimson lipstick,
oh mirror, mirror.

My son slams the door, brings the music
to a boil.

Make a fist, he says. Come on, punch my
stomach, hard.
And leans down to admire himself
in my eyes.

His body sends up
little coiled signals, dark pulses, a code
he can almost read.

PRACTICING

for Benjamin, prestissimo

THE WAY he leans
into it, head to one side, all drama,
the rigging in his neck pulled taut
in the wind of the music.

He's moving fast now
without me, eyes on the page, into
his own depth. And I
can't follow him, though my fingers

keep shaping
the sounds—*they* know
what's next, they've played those
sharps and crescendos, they can still

taste the spray.
His legs pump the pedals, sweaty hands
slip on the keys.
Too fast, he knows it's too fast but

he can't stop, won't, he leans
into it, head down, listening,
as if it were pouring through the rapids,
pounding, calling him where he can't
not go.

LEARNING FIRE

for Jonathan

MY CHILD crawls up against me
with a trapped
animal's cry, barely audible.
His friends at the camp-out crowd around:
Is he on fire? Will his hand turn black?
Will his fingers
fall off?

I fold a towel soaked in ice water
to his swollen fist. In a week, dead skin
will peel in white strips
like eucalyptus bark.

Pain stitches the tattoo
of the new word
into his skin. All night I'm the water that
soothes him, the deadwood the fire
swallows. An all night wind
saws away at a tall tree
in front of our tent. I wake up
shivering

into the matted stir of morning,
a branch in the dirt beside us.
He is all hand.
Light brings back the splayed
tent pegs, the bony ground.

MILKWEED

WHEN THE OLD one gets very old
I come every afternoon.
What cloudy eyes you have,
grandma. What poor
tendril hands.

Milkweed, mother of promises, how
do you live
so thin?
I would have died years ago.

I wait at the brink of the high bed
to be forgiven.
It's chilly here. Let me
cover you, grandma. Go ahead. Die.

She sits up in her white
disguise,
the better to see me.
Her eyes shift and settle: she knows

what I am. Her fingers
take mine in their dry grip
and hang on.
The air is so sharp I can hear
the small twigs snapping.

AT THE OPEN GRAVE

THE PICKAXE hurts. Caked
bedrock,
hard-packed. The pick
goes after rock bottom.

And the gravedigger in his muddy
rubber-soled shoes. Dirt clings
to the rusted metal, clumps of it,
damp from the last rain.
He flicks it off
easily.

Your leftover words, I want to
say them now, break them
into their first
colors: *red* and *purple*,
green. Let the tree fall in that muffled
forest of yours. One of us
will hear it. Well, then. Let it be
half-heard.

You were telling me something.
In this life we bury the dead
alive. What an austere
discipline,
to turn and walk away.

VISION

LAUGHING, I look at myself in the mirror
and see only the eyes.
They take in the whole white distance to the wall,
dilate without blinking, open
the knot of my face.
Suddenly I know I will trade everything for this.

I am leaning against the sink.
Water rushes out of the pipes, icy,
splashes my rings,
my feet on the naked tiles—

I can almost see myself by my own light.

I cover the mirror with my hands.
Wherever I am now, I won't need
even that master.

IN THE LAND OF THE BODY

1

A CROOKED
finger of pain, a hand, a gloved hand
reaches inside me, asking,
Does this hurt? Does this?

I ask it Where next? but it doesn't
know yet. And you

reach for me shyly, as if you
didn't know me,
didn't know either
where to touch. Is this good?
Is this?

Your fingers stutter a little
as if the pain
hurt them. Is this how the rest
                                    begins?
Your mouth, my body staring, and that hand

twisting inside.

2

HE SHOWS ME my body translated
into swirls of light on a fluorescent screen.

This is the thorax with its curving
fingers of rib, its thick
ring of fat. These
are the soft blind organs, huddled, the lungs
filled with black air.
This is a transverse section
of the spinal column: a white eye,
a dark pupil.

I'm waiting for him to read
my fortune:
values on a scale, relative
shades of gray.

Inside me everything's in color, glossy,
opaque. A lump of pain
in a hidden pocket.

His voice segmented, exact, he
talks to the picture,
takes a crayon, draws
a burst of rays
around the star he's discovered

but hasn't named.

3

THE MOMENT the doctor. *Looks like.*
No way to. Scrubbed hands

scooping. *The size of.* At the mercy
of the body. And to carry it

inside for years, sealed,
without even. *But if.* Not to know

your own. *There have been*
cases. Dear God

I don't believe in. But
what would I. *Tuesday.* The sun

leaves its snail's trace across. It's
the waiting that

4

THE GOOD CHILDREN eat what I set before them,
lick the plate clean
and wait

for an answer. Their feet
dangle above the linoleum.
The big one is doodling a whale,

choosing crayons:
Are you going to die? He adds
gray spotted wings.

The little one draws my face on a beanpole
in a garden
of green nails. He gives me

a loopy skirt, shoes
and a few stiff flowers.
When he bends over to color me in,

I see how careful he is
to keep the colors from spilling
over the lines.

5

A SHARP wind
pries at the doorjamb, riddles
the wet sash. Was it just
last week?

We sat at the fireplace, the four of us,
reading *Huck Finn*. I did the Duke,
you the Dauphin, the kids
tossed pillows in the air.
We owned that life.

There's a future loose in my body and I
am its servant:
carrying wood, fetching water.

You cup a hand over my stomach
to feel the dark
dividing.
The hand listens hard.

And the children are practicing
pain: one finger, quick!
through the candle flame.

6

WE HAVE CHOSEN each other.
The stranger walks slowly toward me,
a white mask over his words.

I left everything to come here.
They took away my watch.
The children
grew smaller, disappeared.

Where are we going. I lie down
under the thirsty mouths
of the soundproof ceiling.

This room has no windows, no
shadows. The air
burns cold
and the cold is absolute.

We start off together on the long journey.
My sack of flesh closes around him.
My belly
swallows his hands.

7

MINE IS SMALL and slow-growing,
floats
at an unknown altitude.

When I sleep, the doctors
sway over my bed. They flicker away
and swim up, slippery,
tie my feet down,
cut a vista into my belly.

Everyone lives under a cloud, they say.

Mine chafes the horizon, so small
I will cover it with my hand.

8

AND THEN I rose
to the dazzle of light, to the pine trees
plunging and righting themselves in a furious wind.

To have died and come back again
raw, crackling,
and the numbness
stunned.

That clumsy
pushing and wheeling inside my chest, that ferocious
upturn—
I give myself to it. Why else
be in a body?

Something reaches inside me, finds the pocket
that sewed itself shut, turns it
precipitously
out into the air.

ALONE ON THE MOUNTAIN
on my birthday

I CLIMB up here only
to feel small again. Blue liquor
of distances: one sip and I start to lose
size, anger, the sticky burrs
of wanting. *If only, what if*—let the wind
carry it away.

Wave after wave of shadow comes over
the mountain, like some great
migration. Up here
everything's painted the four
bare colors: sky, cloud, rock, shadow.

To be the object of so much weather!
I'm the only one left at the end
of the last act. Everyone has died,
or gone off to be married.

Look how that tree
catches the wind, strains like a kite against
its patch of sky. That's
what I come for.
                         An important cloud
is making its way to some other mountain, to the sea,
scattering finches like poppyseed.

DEATHS I COME BACK TO

THE LILACS on the roadside are rusting. They hold up
clusters of lost light,
soft brown stars that wrinkle and go dead.

The deaths I keep coming back to
send up a musky smoke, the slow
burn of decay.

On the forest floor, pale vellum leaves;
rain-tempered pine cones, stained with resin;
pine branches drying their brooms, tails, tufts of red;
a half-eaten stump, the corky wood
flaming upward.

Then the creak of a dry branch, that
cawing of deadwood ready to fall.

Dead leaves on the ground, the watery shadows
of the living:
the sift and sway of light.

In the rutted pine tree, rough
stubs of branches go after
the light. I climbed
that tree, too, death after death.

I snap off a branch of hemlock
to carry home, stroking the bright wingtips,
moist green, without memory.

DAY-BLIND

ONE CLAP OF DAY and the dream
rushes back
where it came from. For a moment
the ground is still moist with it.
Then day settles. You step onto dry land.

Morning picks out the four
corners, coffeepot, shawl of dust
on a cupboard. Stunned
by brightness, that dream—
where did it go?

All day you grope in a web
of invisible stars. The day sky soaks them up
like dreams. If you could see
in the light, you'd see what fires
keep spinning, spinning their mesh of threads

around you. They're closer
than you think, pulsing
into the blue. You press your forehead
to the cool glass.

They must be out there in all that dazzle.

ABOUT THE AUTHOR

Chana Bloch was born in New York City and studied at Cornell, Brandeis and the University of California at Berkeley. In addition to her poems, she has published critical essays and a study of George Herbert, as well as translations from the Hebrew of Yehuda Amichai and Dahlia Ravikovitch, and the Yiddish of Isaac Bashevis Singer, Jacob Glatstein and Abraham Sutzkever. Among her awards are the 92nd Street "Y" Discovery Award, an NEA Fellowship in Poetry, an NEH Fellowship, the Book of the Year Award of the Conference on Christianity and Literature, and the Columbia University Translation Center Award. Her translation (in collaboration with Ariel Bloch) of the biblical Song of Songs will be published in 1993. She lives in Berkeley with Ariel Bloch and their two sons, Benjamin and Jonathan, and is Professor of English at Mills College.